Let's Celebrate!

Christopher Cushing

INFOMAX
COMMON CORE
READERS

Rosen
Classroom™

New York

Published in 2013 by The Rosen Publishing Group, Inc.
29 East 21st Street, New York, NY 10010

Book Design: Michael Harmon

Photo Credits: Cover Image Source/Image Source/Getty Images; p. 4 Maria Teijeiro/Digital Vision/Getty Images;
p. 5 Betsie Van der Meer/Stone/Getty Images; p. 6 VisionsofAmerica/JoeSohm/Photodisc/Getty Images;
p. 7 Lori Adamski Peek/The Image Bank/Getty Images; pp. 8, 9, 13 Ariel Skelley/Photographer's Choice/Getty Images;
p. 10 James and James/FoodPix/Getty Images; p. 11 (fireworks) Samba Photo/Samba Photo/Getty Images;
p. 11 (family) Ariel Skelley/Blend Images/Getty Images; p. 12 Paul Harris/Stone/Getty Images;
p. 14 Thinkstock/Comstock Images/Getty Images; p. 16 (earth) Stocktrek/Digital Vision/Getty Images.

ISBN: 978-1-4488-8962-4
6-pack ISBN: 978-1-4488-8963-1

Manufactured in the United States of America

CPSIA Compliance Information: Batch #WS12RC: For further information contact Rosen Publishing, New York, New York at 1-800-237-9932.

Word Count: 126

Contents

Let's Celebrate! 4

Earth Day 6

Mother's Day 8

The Fourth of July 10

Halloween 12

Happy Birthday! 14

Time to Celebrate! 15

Words to Know 16

Index 16

Do you know what it means to celebrate?

When we celebrate, we come together
to honor someone or something.

Earth Day is in April.

How do you celebrate Earth Day?

We do nice things for Earth.

We plant a tree!

Mother's Day is in May.

How do you celebrate Mother's Day?

We do nice things for our mom.

We give our mom a big hug!

We give her flowers, too!

The Fourth of July is our nation's birthday.
How do you celebrate the Fourth of July?

We wave American flags.

We watch fireworks!

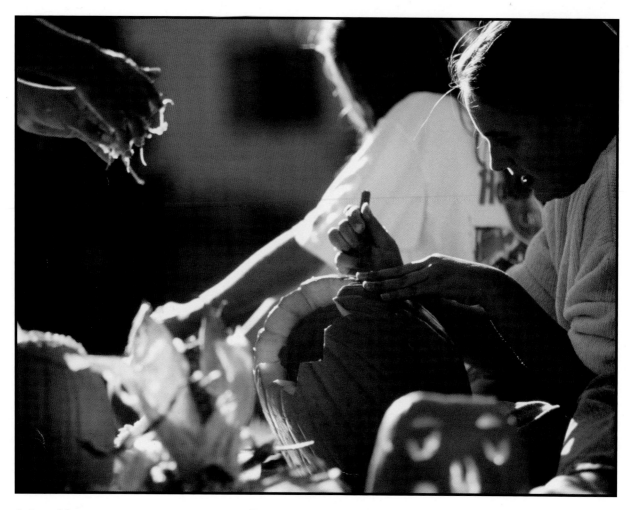

Halloween is in October.

How do you celebrate Halloween?

We put on fun clothes.

People give us candy!

How do you celebrate your birthday?

Do you have a party?

Do you eat cake?

Time to Celebrate!

Earth Day ⟶ April

Mother's Day ⟶ May

Fourth of July ⟶ July

Halloween ⟶ October

Words to Know

Earth

fireworks

flag

Index

birthday, 10, 14

candy, 13

Earth, 7

Earth Day, 6, 15

fireworks, 11

flags, 11

Fourth of July, 10, 15

Halloween, 12, 15

mom, 9

Mother's Day, 8, 15